Unusual Aspects
of Avebury

Published by
Robert LaMont

Copyright   R. LaMont & A. Hedderman

ISBN 0-9538656-1-4 (2nd revised)
(ISBN 0-9538656-0-6 1st edition)

Cover design by A. Hedderman
Cover Production by R. LaMont

Typeset by R. LaMont

Printed and bound in Great Britain by
The Shires Press Unit 2-3
Shails Lane Industrial Park
River Way Trowbridge
Wiltshire BA14 8NS.

This Guide is dedicated to every race colour and creed that will visit Avebury, who view the world around them with new eyes.

The sudden opening of one's eyes to the elaborate extravagant beauty around us gives life to imagination.
The re-discovery of the Sunset wishing the day farewell.
The three hundred million galaxies above.
The intricacy of the present moment.
This is all the wealth we need.
The Scientist, the poet, and the philosopher.
All describing the same grand artistry of existence.
Compose your thoughts in quiet contemplation.
Publish them in your silent mind
Unfold the truth, repeat them as dreams.
Understand them as love, now just listen to the silent song of your own soul.
Above all, enjoy your journey.

Contents

v

Page

FOLLOWED BY

Alternative Guide to Life display and classified

section, these pages contain information and contact details to

help you find alternative means to a better understanding of

health, life and inner peace.

INTRODUCTION

Treasure comes in many different forms. Thousands of years have passed since our Neolithic ancestors erected the stones. Many have speculated on reasons why such sites exist. This guide attempts to educate, with fun, the contemporary views while helping you discover those aspects of Avebury you may find almost mystical in nature.

What this guidebook shows you

Many of the stones contain hidden images that are formed from the natural surface of the stones, some by the play of light and shadows, others by the formation of lichen made from fungus and algae a symbiosis that takes many years to establish itself on the stones.

Adults and Children alike will find this guidebook one of the most stimulating. We thought a type of treasure hunt would keep everyone interested while educating you on the established archaeological information. We have attempted to collect some of the best examples that can be seen at almost any time of the day.

Simulacra

(an image or representation of something).
Have you ever made shapes out of the clouds? Seen images in different patterns. These form part of the main concept of this publication and attempt to make it fun. This is not an alternative to the established views, it works in conjunction with them and we hope it will make your visit to Avebury an interesting one.

While you certainly see your own images, those contained here are some of the most spectacular. The younger adults (and some older ones) will have hours of interesting educational fun. We hope you enjoy your quest to find the **Unusual Aspects of Avebury**. You are free to decided whether the images are intentional or coincidence, the idea here is just to make you look a little closer at the individual parts to Europe's oldest and largest stone circle.

Circle Map

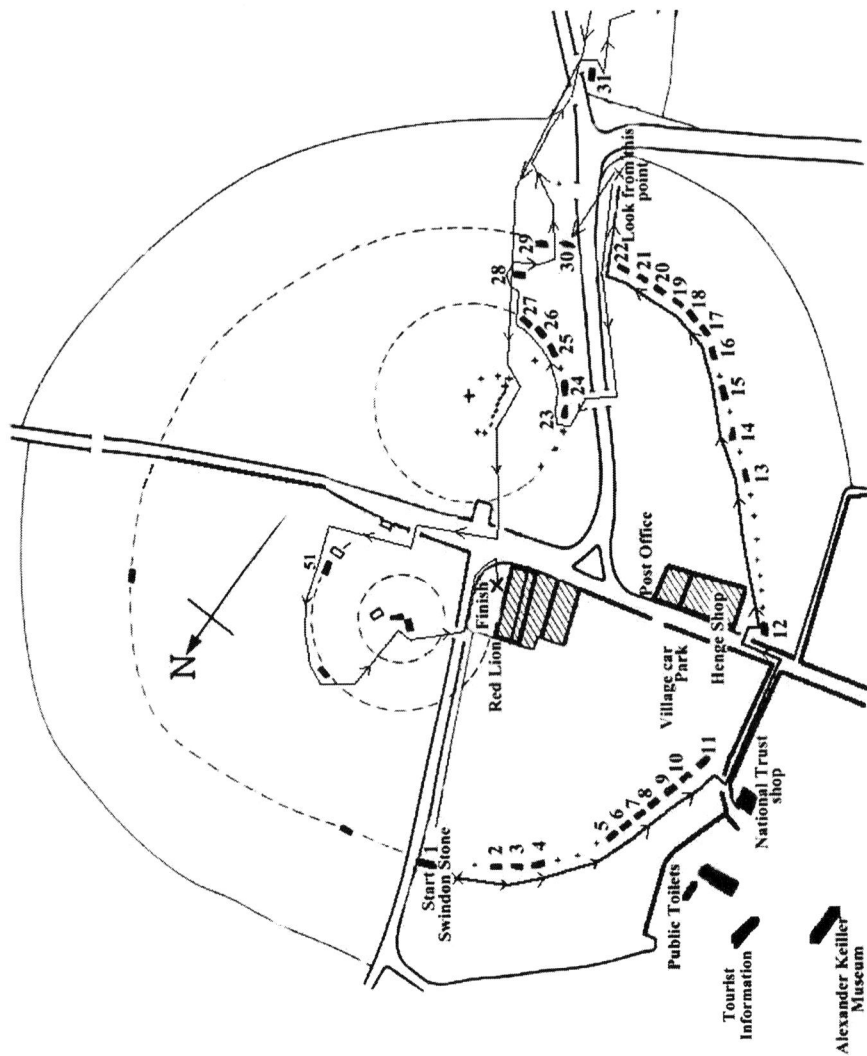

N

Start 1
Swindon Stone
2
3
4
5
6 7 8 9
10
11
Red Lion
Finish
51
0

23
24
25 26
27
28
29
30
31
Look from this point
22 21
20
19
18
17
16
15
14
13
12

Post Office
Village car Park
Henge Shop
National Trust shop
Public Toilets
Tourist Information
Alexander Keiller Museum

Fig 1

From the Red Lion car park take the Swindon Road and enter the first gate on your left. The largest stone in front of you is your starting point, The Swindon Stone. (See map for details.) This stone has many facets, we don't intend to give you all the information, some you can clearly see for yourself. What you need to do is look for noses, eyes, mouths etc. When you find one part of a face look for the corresponding parts.

Make your way past the modern concrete marker to the next stone. We do assure you it gets more interesting as we continue this unique tour of Avebury.

Information snippet

According to legend Geoffrey of Monmouth, a medieval monk with a passion for tall stories told of how Merlin the magician moved Stonehenge from a mountain in Ireland by sea and river. These bluestones have been identified as coming from that region.

Fig 2

This is a wonderful example of multiple images to be found in one stone. As you can clearly see the main character seems to be looking up from the left with his eyes closed, nose and mouth clearly defined. But take a closer look lower down on what you would call his chin, another image starts to come to life. It does not stop there, moving your gaze but keeping your position, down to the right there seems to be a very unhappy chap with a large mouth small nose and closed eyes. To the right the ear is formed by the indent, the forehead and face line are two distinct colours facing to the right. (A large pixie maybe?)

Info Snippet

As you look at the stone from this angle you can just see the entrance to Avebury Manor. Well kept gardens and a wealth of history have made this a very important part of the local landscape. Such names as Sir William Flanders-Petrie, John Aubrey, William Stukeley and poet laureate Sir John Betjeman have all walked the halls of the Manor.

4

The next five stones we could find no distinctive images that would grab your attention. Then again could you? Remember this tour is best described like beauty, it's all in the eye of the beholder. If you check your map we have jumped to fig 8, this is where we will continue.

Fig 8

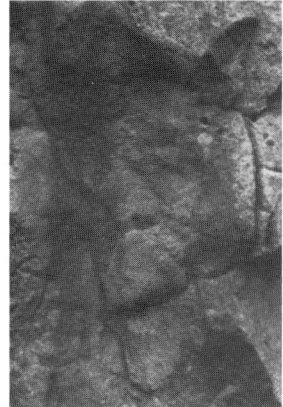

This is not the only hidden image here but like all the others it will take a while before you begin to see what is in front of you.

Strange how almost all the faces seem to have a masculine quality about them. Do you think our ancient ancestors knew something that we still don't?

Again you will see multiple faces here, to give you a hand look on the left side (they all seem to be old men). Moving over to the right the large nose gives you the point to start constructing the other face.

The indent slightly off centre to the right and leaning into the left gives you a third face. Again, many more could be seen given your position, the light, and shadow. Take a few moments to check for more.

Once more we have left you to see if you can find anything of interest in the next stone. Don't think there may not be any images because we could not find any ourselves.
Our next image is marked on your map as **fig 10.**

This is one of our favourite images we hope you can clearly see the alien know as "A Grey" in the middle of the stone. His eyes are quite distinctive and the line of his jaw leads you down to his small straight mouth. There is no point in trying to look for his nose, for apparently they don't really have one. There is another image to the bottom left, try to see if you can make that one out.

Fig 10

One last stone remains in this section, again we could not see anything that really struck us but now that you have got into the right mood you may be more successful. (Fig 12 on your map).

This publication is not designed to give an in-depth view on the archaeological aspects of Avebury. Anyone wishing to further understand the established aspects should purchase the appropriate books or visit the following outlets.

National Trust shop
As you would expect at any National Trust outlet items are of fine quality and a great way to commemorate your visit to Avebury. Membership details can be gained from friendly efficient staff, entitling you to discounted access to hundreds of National Trust buildings across the country.

Getting to the end of this section you proceed out of the gate and down the steps. You have the choice, turn **right** it will lead you to:

The Alexander Keiller Museum
Converted from a stable the museum houses interesting finds from the surrounding area. Based mainly on the daily life of the inhabitants of the area of almost five thousand years ago.

West Kennet Long Barrow, The Sanctuary, Silbury Hill, The Circles & the Avenue of stones all feature in the displays.

Turn **left** in front of the National Trust shop and follow the road out onto the village High Street. Across the road and slightly to your left you can see the next leg of your tour and from this position...

The Henge shop. Covering an array of items for all tastes, the Henge shop is situated opposite the local car park in the High Street, the post office next door also serves as a small provisions store.

Walking across the High Street make your way through the gate and onto the next stone in our tour. Remember that as you get into the swing of things you will start to see your own images. Now look to the first stone and begin the next section of this unusual tour.

Approach the first stone. This stone has been damaged in the past and partially broken up to use for building's, mainly the church and dovecote. What has been left in this stone leaves an impression of a "happy shark" (fig 12), swimming up from the earth. You can distinctly see the eye and grinning mouth on the north east face of the stone.

Fig 12

Info Snippet

One of the interesting theories about the stones is that they are made up of male and female forms. This can be seen in all areas, the simple rule for observation is that the wide stones are female and the tall ones are male. (Local lore states that the male ones you can climb and the female ones you can't, surprising!).

Move on to the next stone. Take your time with this unhappy fellow, as you wander round this stone look for a small dark eye, once you have found this step back and look at the whole face you should notice the drooping mouth a small nose and a slightly jutting chin.

We couldn't see any faces in the next two stones (marked as figs 14 &15). This does not mean that you won't be able to, so take your time looking at these to see if we have missed any.

Fig 13

If you now move on to the stone marked as **fig 16** on your map you will meet this strange looking chap. Two of natures sculptures came to mind when viewing from the angle shown here. First, the slanted eyes, thick lips and Roman nose makes this large face obvious (we think). He seems to have that look, you know the one that gives you the impression he knows something we don't, standing in that spot for so long he probably does.

Fig 16

Second, if you take the whole stone, the top section as represents the head & the large section of stone to the left acts as his shield. You may now begin to see what we have called "The knight of Stone". Maybe you can see more but it makes a good starting point for your imagination to blossom with this fine example.

Fig 22

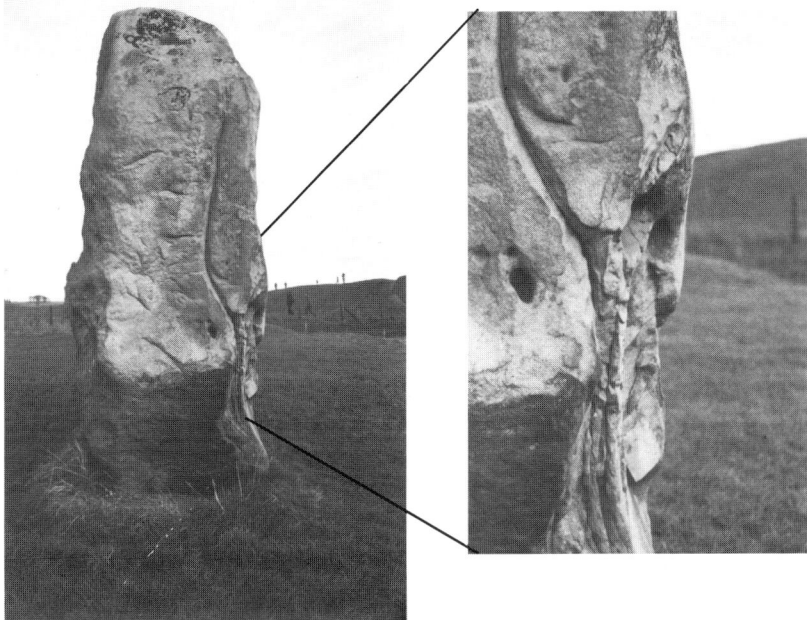

Fig 21

When you reach the last two stones in this section, you should be able to see two very stern chaps looking at you. We call these two "The Bouncers". So if you misbehave, expect these two chaps to up stones and bounce you out of the area.

The first of the two is looking directly at you as you approach it from around the circle. He has probably been watching you for some time. The other bouncer is lower down in the stone and is looking out over the Avenue.

Before you make your way out of the gate to the other side of the road. Take a walk over towards the other side of the ditch, check the map for the actual view point. Look carefully at the stone marked on the map as **fig 30.** This stone is known as the devils chair or kings stone. Many people sit on what you can now see as his chin from this angle. The face of a man, not too dissimilar than that of Christ looking Eastward. The long hair, closed eye and distinctive nose make up an image that does seem to command a certain respect.

Fig 30

This image and a detailed account of it's mythology can be gleaned from a wonderful publication; "Legendary Landscapes" by J. D. Wakefield. A recent local publication describing, not just this particular stone but many interesting aspects concerning Wiltshire. I am grateful to the author for pointing out this wonderful face to me.

If you now make your way back towards the gate leading across the road we will continue once you reach the other side. Make your way into the next quadrant of the circle complex and the first in the next series is in front of you slightly to your left. (Numbered 23 on your map).

You should be able to see "Nelly" the elephant. As you look at the stone the right hand side is her trunk with the top left as her ear. She looks as if she is taking a drink of water. This is known locally as the "Elephant Stone". This has also had extensive research by the co-author of this publication.

Mirrored onto itself it resembles the Great Sphinx of Egypt. The wider aspects appear in the Sphinx guide, purchased from The Red Lion.

Fig 23

Info Snippet
Considering the style of this guide it would not be out of place to suggest that there may have been some sort of global communication via certain types of trade, as far back as 4,000 years ago.

This idea is not usually welcomed by the established views but forensic science has found evidence to indicate trade between Egypt and the Americas long before Columbus. Cocaine traces found in the mummified body of Ramses II along with nicotine fragments seem to indicate a trade between both continents at a time when this was thought impossible.

Lectures can be arranged on this unique aspect of the stones and other historic anomalies via The Red Lion by the Co-author of this publication.
E-mail rob333@btinternet.com

Stone 24 on your map has been left for you to have fun with, all we will say is that if you are very careful you will see a face.

Moving onto the next megalith, our magical mystery tour of Avebury continues.

Fig 25 The Ram;
Why the Ram we hear you say, well if you walk towards the road then turn around you will see its eye above a long straight nose on the right hand side, with the rams horn curving over the eye and around the head. Don't worry we don't think the Ram is going to charge....

Fig 25

Info Snippet
Before we leave this part of the inner circles it is interesting to note that once an obelisk stood 6.4m high, now marked by a concrete plinth. Interestingly the shadow (given it's height) would have struck the set of smaller stones you can see forming a "D" shape. A Neolithic clock to possibly indicate religious time table, planting of crops and sacrifices. No one really knows the actual purpose of this "clock".

Fig 29

Having already looked at the 30th stone from the vantage point across the road, we come to the last stone we have for you in this area. This does not mean you will not see any more images here, you are probably very good at it by now. It would take the fun out of your stroll around Avebury if you were given all the possibilities. This unhappy looking stone cruncher seems to project a look that he's not too happy being left there. Ah well, they say people get grouchy when they get old and 4,000 years is plenty of time to get grouchy!

Now walk towards the bank (towards the trees) over the top and to your right go through the gate, cross the road and enter the avenue.

Avenue Map

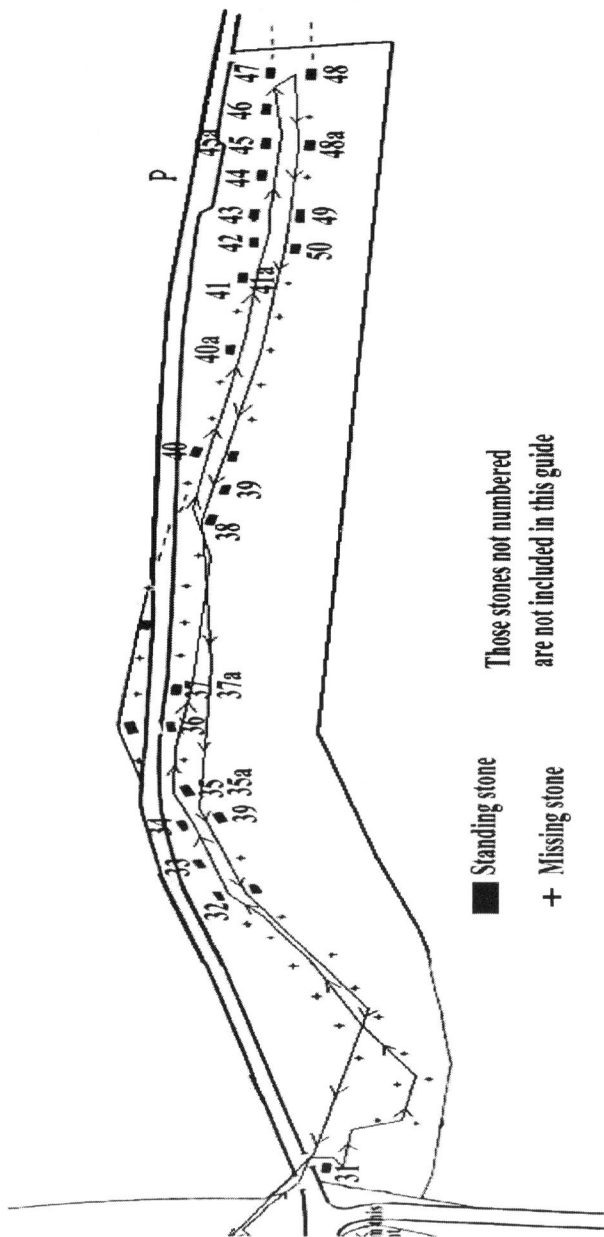

Standing stone

+ Missing stone

Those stones not numbered
are not included in this guide

16

Fig 31

Fig 31

From this vantage point you could be forgiven for thinking you are looking at a huge carving. If the stones could talk I wonder what tales they would tell. What sights they may have seen in that four thousand year history. A time span that would cover our entire knowledge of modern man. Easter Island statues seem to come to mind when observing this stone. what do you think? Standing here allows wonderful views of both the circles and the Avenue, just take a moment to soak up the atmosphere before moving on to the next stone.

Info snippet

If you stand on the Kings Stone chin (devils chair) fig 30, a person of average height can see the top of Silbury hill. Could this be deliberate? Could this be an early warning system for imminent attacks or management of the processions that took place? Could the height of Silbury have been dictated by this? Considering the height of Wanes hill in between the two points, it would seem likely.

Walk up the Avenue towards the top of the hill. There is a five stone gap before you get to the next stone; you will notice the Avenue crosses over the road then back again. We will not be taking you across the road. The next stone we include is marked on your map as **Fig 35**.

Fig 35

This stone has two figures that are visible. The first one is seen looking toward the stone with your back to the road, you should be able to see a young lady with long hair, holding her head in her hands, what she is contemplating nobody knows. You could also be forgiven for seeing that it may have a primate quality about it looking to the left. As with all our images you may see something completely different but that's what makes this guide so much fun.

Fig 35a

If you walk around the stone to the other side, you will be able to see our friend "Morn", a rather glum looking fellow with a flat face looking away from the circle down the rest of the avenue. He has a small eye, a flat nose and a straight mouth with dimples. As we were contemplating the images to be included in this publication it seemed impossible to choose simply because everyone will see something different. If you need some time to yourselves then we hope this will help you give the younger adults time to play detective leaving you with the silence of the stones.

In this particular run of stones we could not find images that would stand out for reproduction in this guide. You may have better luck, the stones marked on your map 32, 33, 34, see if you can find your own images.

Fig 36
Move further down the Avenue to the next stone. If you stand with the stone between you and the road you will be able to see the "Happy Gent" looking up into the sky. His nose, mouth and forehead are quite visible on the left-hand side of the stone.

Fig 36

The image below can be found by walking to the next stone. With your back to the road, halfway down on the left. He is a serious looking gentleman, (maybe he didn't like the Romans invading his land, maybe he's got a headache, who knows?)

Fig 37

Following the line indicated on your map continue to make your way towards the lower regions of the avenue.

The next stone we have examined for you will be on your right hand side. It is stone 38 on your map.

Fig 38
This stone we have named "The Maiden". If you approach the stone so that you are looking south down the avenue. You will see the outline of a woman walking towards you with a bundle under her left arm and her head covered in a cloak.

Info snippet
One of many Arthurian legends the transformation from "The Hag" into a beautiful maiden. This came about when Sir Gawain kissed his betrothed, an old hag whom he had agreed to marry in order to save Arthur's life. She had given him the answer to a question posed to him by a mystical knight. Had he not answered correctly Arthur would have been killed. On Sir Gawain's wedding night the hag asked for a kiss. With fear and loathing Sir Gawain kissed her and transformed into a vision of beauty. Perhaps we have that maiden frozen in stone?

Moving on to the stone marked as **fig 39.** on your map (the next stone on the same side of the avenue).

If you look carefully you may find more than the three images we have highlighted below. See if you can find them without us giving the clues as to where. In the process we have left one distinctive face out. Can you find it?
(An alien may have leaned over and left his mark in the stone.)

Fig 39

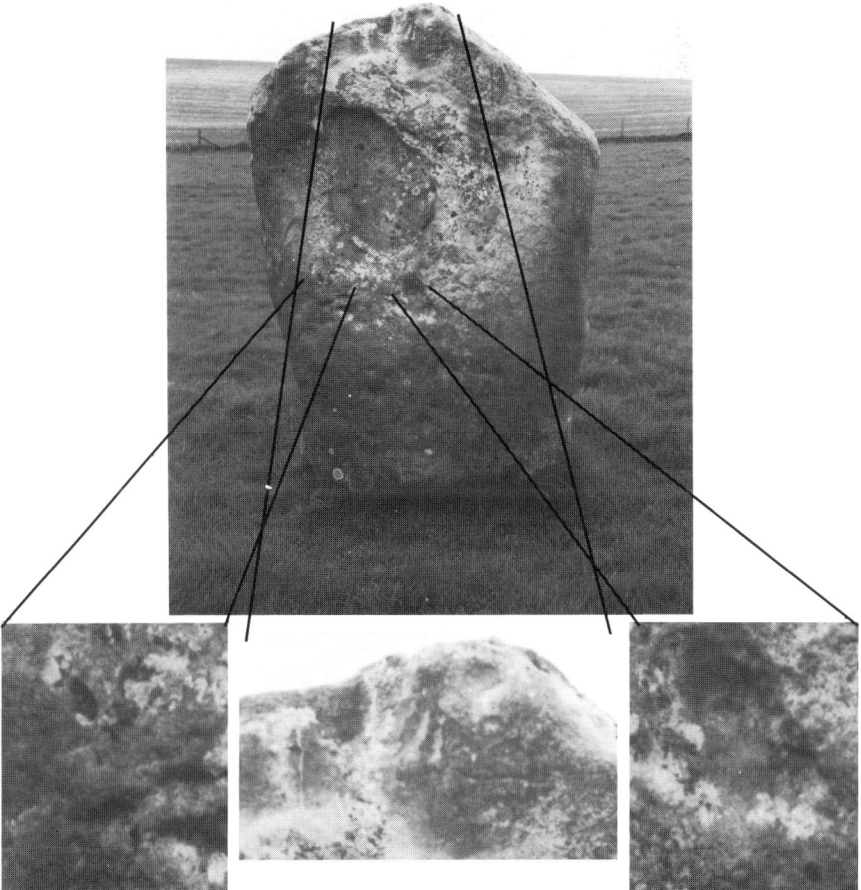

Fig 40

Now walk across to the other side of the Avenue our next sculpture is **fig 40.** on your map. You can't help but think that this happy looking face was deliberately carved but on closer inspection you can clearly see it's a natural feature. There could be a case for previous desecration resulting in this wonderful example of simulacra but this again would only be speculation.

Staying on the same side of the avenue make your way down past the next stone and past **fig 40a.** stay on the left hand side as you go down, arriving at the final row of the next seven stones.

Fig 41

Fig 41a

Fig 41 (Baby Elephant)

Go to the first stone on the left and walk round it until you can look back at it towards the road, what you have here is "Long Nose" with its large eye to the left of its trunk like nose and a small mouth below. If you look a little closer the trunk becomes a nose with the mouth under it. Halfway up the long nose a darker patch appears forming an eye with a few ageing lines. Completing the picture of a man with a Roman nose is the elongated forehead. We are sure you can find more.

Fig 41a (Woman in the Moon)

Stay with the same stone just walk around it until you can see the "Woman in the Moon". Notice the distinct shape of the face within the half moon curve in the stone. It just looked more feminine than masculine.

Fig 42

Onto the next stone, this one does a good impression of a rabbit hence the fact we have named him "Bugs", You will be able to see him as you walk towards him, keeping the road on your left.

He is facing the road with his ears up and alert for trouble. If you manage to get the exact angle it does appear quite fearsome.

Fig 43

The next stone we have named "Kong" after the infamous gorilla King Kong. Walk round the stone until you are facing the road and looking up the hill slightly, you will see the square face with the ridged eyebrow, nose and jaw. If the rest of his body was as big as his head he could well be King Kong.

My co-author insists that it looks more like a giant pigs head, with a large snout and mouth. It seems to have a slight smile on it's face. This just goes to show that even we, in production of this guide cannot always see what the other does. Confirming the fact that there are no right or wrong answers. Maybe you will not be able to picture either image but find a completely different one, again that's absolutely fine.

Fig 42

Fig 43

Fig 44

Fig 44
Moving onto the next stone you will see "The Toff", keeping the stone between you and the road, look at the left hand side of the stone you will see his stuck up nose with his smirking mouth below, his eyes are closed. You could imagine him sniffing the wine glass appreciating the delicate bouquet. Talking of wine....

Info Snippet
The Red Lion Inn was granted it's licence in 1822. This was the first licensed premises since the closure of The Catherine Wheel almost a century earlier. The large stone wheel you will see in what is now the car park was a large cider press. No building of this age circa 17th century would be complete without it's constant reports of ghostly happenings. One of the village wells forms part of the internal decor and is said to have been the final resting place of an unfortunate maiden. She has allegedly been seen standing on the stairs by several customers, previous landlords and staff.

Continue on to the next stone fig 45 on your map walk around to the other side and turn to find "Elvis". The king of rock and roll has not left the building, he's here in Avebury, resting. He still has his teddy boy hair style, dark brooding eyes, nose and pouting mouth. Fancy the Neolithic people knowing Elvis would grace our land (excuse the pun) so far into the future. Perhaps you can think of some song titles that may be appropriate given it's location and history. We could only think of two, Jailhouse Rock and Hard Headed Woman. Bad, we know, but can you do better ?

Info snippet
When you get back into the village, as you browse the antique shop you can cast your imagination back to a time when this was the village shop. At one time (1918) it also had a small hotel attached to it and refreshment rooms. The only places left now to sample good food is The Red Lion and Stones restaurant in the courtyard by the National Trust shop. (see directory in the back of this guide).

Fig 45

Fig 45a

Fig 45a
Makes one wonder who inspired who, we have called the back of this stone "The Thinker" as you can see for obvious reasons. Most sculptors will tell you that the image is already contained within the material their skill lies in their ability to remove the excess and reveal the art underneath. We would suggest that nature has always inspired artists, this monolith is no exception. Sitting for 4,000 years in quiet contemplation we can only guess what thoughts are running through his head.

Info Snippet
Construction of Silbury Hill commenced in late summer, almost 5,000 years ago. The accuracy in determining the exact time of year comes from the ants. This may be a strange way to date but in all seriousness the ants that have been found "locked" into the substructure of Silbury have wings getting ready for their late summer mating flights. No one really knows why the hill was built but plenty have their own speculations, and still do. Personally we feel it played a dual role. A religious plateau and part of the South West beacon system. Again just speculation until more empirical evidence comes to light.

Fig 46
The next stone has two smaller faces at the bottom right, one above the other. You should look for a human skull above the face of a cat. These are more difficult to see than before so look carefully. The eye of the skull and the mouth and nose of the cat are the easiest to see.

Info snippet
It is sad to note that most of the three hundred stones that made up the circle and the two avenues were broken down over the years to construct houses and walls in the village. One of the biggest construction jobs made predominately from the original stones was the church that now shows evidence of this. It looks like the Christians of the time removed the pagan worship but adding insult to injury build their own house of worship. This is reminiscent of the Spanish arrival in Mexico placing their churches atop the pyramids. It's refreshing to see that in this modern age insurrection has given way to tolerance.

Whom does the Grail serve?

Fig 47

Fig 47

Moving onto the last stone on the left, you come to "Merlin" or "The Gatekeeper", like all legends of history he is eternal. He is best seen as you walk toward him from the last stone, look for a cloaked figure standing silently, his nose is the only part of his face visible, the rest hidden by his hood. He has stood guard over the Avenue of stones for thousands of years, only awakening when King Arthur called for him, returning to rest after Arthur had moved on. He awaits the time when the world needs him again. His legend lives on in all who take the time to see his image.

If you want to know more about the legend of King Arthur & Merlin the Henge shop in the village of Avebury has various books on the subject. Alternatively you can make a visit to Glastonbury and the fabled isle of Avalon.

Fig 48

Fig 48
With your back to Merlin, look to the stone across from him to find his
Cat waiting patiently for his master to wake up. No wizard would be
complete without his familiar (a term used to describe a magical
companion). As you look at the stone his nose and mouth are on the left,
his eyes are open and his ears are flattened slightly. He is alert for any
signs of his master waking.

As you move up the other side of the avenue back towards Avebury
village we have missed the next stone. This is to give you another chance
to see if your tour of natures sculptures has now given you the eyes to see
your own images.

Info Snippet.
One of the culprits of the destruction of the stones was a medieval barber-
surgeon. He was crushed by one of the megaliths in the act of it's
destruction. Coins found on his body dated his attempt to 1325.
Some of the Avenue stones were re-erected in the 1930's. Many stones
still remain underground. Maybe at some distant time the remaining
stones will be given their rightful place in the circles and Avenue
standing proud for another thousand years or more.

Fig 49

Walk back up the avenue, missing out the next stone and continue onto "Old Bignose" sleeping in the open air. As you approach the stone, you will see his huge protruding hooked nose pointing towards you. His mouth is set in a wry grin and his eyes are closed against the weather. Please be quiet as you walk by, as you do not want to wake him, he may get grumpy.

Fig 49

Info Snippet

Silbury Hill and West Kennet Long Barrow became the first two ancient monuments to be protected by an Act of Parliament in 1883. The National Trust purchased most of the land that makes up the Avenues and prehistoric circle in 1942. The upkeep of the stones became the responsibility of the Office of Works, now known as English Heritage.

Fig 50

Fig 50

Now the next stone you come to has a much smaller face set into it. Walk round the stone so that your back is to the road. Now look towards the left of the stone. About a third of the way up you should see his nose, his eye is slightly up and to the right with his mouth below. If you look carefully you will be able to see his teeth.

We have almost come to the end of this unique tour of the sacred stones. We hope you have had fun and also found it informative. Take a moment to study the map, the position of the stones indicate a belief strong enough to motivate possibly thousands, to work together in order to erect such a vast complex. Given the overall size of the Avenue and Circles it would seem that even as far back as 4,000 years ago, large scale projects encompassing a co-ordination of labour, shelter, food and planning, denotes a more ordered society than we may normally give our ancestors credit.

If you now your way back towards the circles in the village we are going to enter the last section, called the cove. This is the North East quadrant of the circle and contains one of the most spectacular examples of simulacra.

As you make you way back down the Avenue consider a few more facts about the construction of this ancient stone circle.

Avebury with it's 247 standing stones, making up the total originally erected in the circles is unparalleled by any other. In addition to those, another 97 pairs of stones made up the West Kennet avenue (where you are now).

The ditch, although excavated still remains somewhat filled by silt and centuries of rubbish. The original depth was between 7-10m, the width at it's top edge is 23.4m. The great circle has a diameter of 347.4m (1140ft). It encloses an area of approximately 29 acres. The two inner circles can enclose the whole of Stonehenge. The Northern inner circle is 48.7m. Stonehenge has a radius of only 29.5m by comparison.

The scale of this construction, considering the resources available was unbelievable but here we have one of the finest examples of Neolithic engineering on the planet. The privilege is ours to enjoy and we hope you have seen an unexpected side to Avebury.

Fig 51
Now let us get to the last leg of this tour and you will see why we have called this "Medusas stone of souls".

Make your way to the Antique shop and walk down Green Lane. You will pass the church constructed out of the broken Sarsen stones on your right. Walk across the road and enter the last quadrant of the circle. As you can see the stone on the next page has many faces trapped in it's structure, hence the name. Just how many can you see? We have pointed out a few but we suspect there will be more.

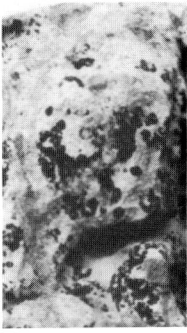

Fig 51

This is the last stone we have featured, look at the top right of the stone to see the distinct facial features of someone looking intently down on you. The insets show you what immediately comes into view from only one angle.

We are sure you can now find more, after all, you should be experts in the art of finding simulacra images. We hope you enjoyed your walk around Avebury, if you make your way back down towards the village crossroads why not stop in at the Red Lion and get some well earned food and drink. You will find another aspect of unusual Avebury on the bar.

The following pages contain the Alternative-Aspects of life guide. We added this section to help you find like-minded people and assist in locating alternative information, we hope you find it useful and we really hope you enjoyed your walk.

Alternative Aspects of Life directory

The following pages contains information on many types of Alternative Aspects to life, spiritual healing and pagan interests. Shops, Hotels, Healers, therapists, Homeopathy and spiritual retreats. We hope you find the following pages almost as interesting as our guide here.

Inclusion in this directory does not mean we have been able to check out every advertiser, we recommend like all initial contact, you make your own enquires as to the claims of the advertiser. We accept no responsibility as to the validity of the advertisers qualifications or claimes.

Enjoy the rest of this guide book, and we hope you find it helpful for future reference.

36

EMBODIMENT

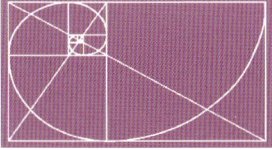

'Practice in Being
Being in Practice'

Courses'
Workshops &
Treatment sessions
for
Personal Harmony and Effective Living

Body Harmony
'A bridge from where you are to where you want to be'
Healing body work accessing the body's own inner wisdom through a 'listening touch'.
Treatments, classes and workshops for personal use & professional certification.
Teaching sessions Support and Development Group

WWW.bodyharmony.com

Usui Shiki Ryoho
Reiki self healing, easily shared with others.
Treatment, First and Second Degree Classes. Master training by apprenticeship only.
Sharing Group
www.usuireiki.com

Shell Essences
Vibrational essences from Australia using homeopathic principals. Treatment only

www.shellessences.com.au
For Further information or Appointments Contact
Kit Ford-Young
Flat 3, Copper Beech, Magdalene St, Glastonbury, Somerset BA6 9EJ
Tel/Fax +44 (0)1458 833250
New Venues and organisers Welcome

WWW.ALTERNATIVE-ASPECTS.COM

The best way to describe our new web site

Is to ask if you have ever had an interest in the following subjects

CRYSTAL HEALING ; SPIRITUAL AWAKENING ; HYPNOSIS ; PARANORMAL ; UFO'S ;
CROPCIRCLES ; STONE CIRCLES ; ANCIENT MYSTERIES ; PAGAN WAYS ; PYRAMIDS ; POWER
OF THE MIND ; STAR SIGNS ; AND MUCH MORE… ALTERNATIVE HEALING
WWW.ALTERNATIVE-ASPECTS.COM

WWW.ALTERNATIVE-ASPECTS.COM

The best way to describe our new web site

Is to ask if you have ever had an interest in the following subjects

CRYSTAL HEALING ; SPIRITUAL AWAKENING ; HYPNOSIS ; PARANORMAL ; UFO'S ; CROPCIRCLES ; STONE CIRCLES ; ANCIENT MYSTERIES ; PAGAN WAYS ; PYRAMIDS ; POWER OF THE MIND ; STAR SIGNS ; AND MUCH MORE…….

ALTERNATIVE TRAVEL	ALTERNATIVE HEALING
ALTERNATIVE THEORIES	ALTERNATIVE HISTORY
ALTERNATIVE ARCHAEOLOGY	ALTERNATIVE FUTURE!!

Here is an opening offer to help launch our new site

WWW.ALTERNATIVE-ASPECTS.COM

We can act as your shop window on the world !!! If you have a product or service and have access to a computer then why not get new clients or sell your products via the net and mail order? If you have an internet account (e.mail) but no web site, this is for you.

1. Make contact and tell us what you are thinking about doing. (alternative).
2. We will design and upload your new web page to our site.
3. You pay a "one-off" fee of just £40.00 for design and just £10.00 per month to have a shop window on the world. It's that simple but there is much more...

WHAT DO YOU GET FOR £10.00 PER MONTH ?

We will make every effort to increase and maintain the number visiting our site, viewing your pages. We will be logged with, not just the well know Euro-American search-engines but Japan, Australia, central and south America. We will also set up your own E-mail account FREE. **Yourname@alternative-aspects.com.** This will allow you to communicate with your interested clients privately. If you can do credit card transactions, even better you will make a good living. If you can't, don't worry, we will help you process the credit card transactions so you can be sure instantly via e.mail your stock has been paid for and checked. IT WILL LOOK LIKE YOUR OWN BUSINESS CAN TAKE CC ORDERS. There is a small fee to cover transaction charges.

To get in contact with us about your very own web page just E.Mail us at the following address **rob333@btinternet.com. or alistairh@lycos.com**

Think about how much just the local paper would charge, then think how many people use the World Wide Web. **For £10.00 your can have the WORLD, wide web** .All you need to take up this offer is a current E.Mail address.

Let the numbers speak for themselves;

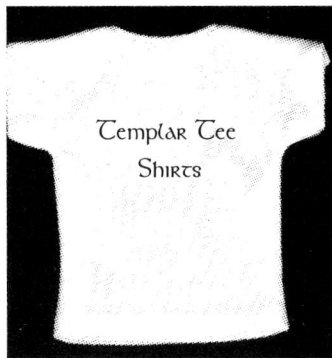

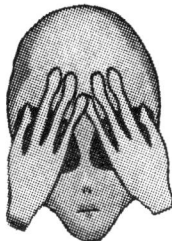

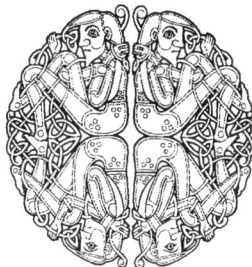

42

College of Integrated Chinese Medicine	Yuan Traditional College Ltd
College of Integrated Chinese Medicine 19 Castle Street, Reading RG1 7SB Tel: 0118 950 8880 Fax: 0118 950 8890 www.cicm.org.uk	**Yuan Traditional College Ltd** 7A Clapham High Street, London. SW4 7TS Tel/Fax: 020-7622 9079

College of Integrated Chinese Medicine
19 Castle Street, Reading
RG1 7SB
Tel: 0118 950 8880 Fax: 0118 950 8890
www.cicm.org.uk

The College of Traditional Acupuncture
Tao House, Queensway,Leamington Spa, Warwickshire, CV31 3LZ
Tel: 01926 422121
Fax: 01926 888282
www.acupuncture-coll.ac.uk

The London College of Traditional Acupuncture and Oriental Medicine
HR House, 447 High Road, London. N12 0AZ
Tel: 020-8371 0820
Fax: 020-8371 0830
www.lcta.com

Norma (COmplex Homeopathy) Limited
Unit 3, 1-16 Hollybrook Road,
Upper Shirley, Southampton. SO16 6RB
Tel: 023-8077 0513
Fax: 023-8070 2459

Northern College of Acupuncture
61 Mickelgate, York. YO1 6LJ
Tel: 01904 343305
Fax: 01904 330370
www.chinese-medicine.co.uk

The South West College of Oriental Medicine
PO Box 795, Bristol, BS99 5WZ
Tel/Fax: 0117-907 8891
www.swcom.org.uk

Wessex College of Natural and Complementary Medicine
128 New Road, Copnor,
Portsmouth, PO2 7RJ
023-9282 8998

Yuan Traditional College Ltd
7A Clapham High Street,
London. SW4 7TS
Tel/Fax: 020-7622 9079

The Society of Teachers of the Alexander Technique (STAT)
129 Camden Mews, London. NW1 9AH
Tel: 020-7284 3338 Fax: 020-7482 5435
www.stat.org.uk

TheInstitute of Traditional Herbal Medicine and Aromatherapy
Regents College, London.
Tel: 01206 393465
Fax: 01206 393522
www.aromatherapy-studies.com

Faculty of Astrological Studies
BM 7470, London. WC1N 3XX
Tel: 07000 790143
www.astrology.org.uk

The College of Ayurveda (UK)
20 Annes Grove, Great Linford,
Milton Keynes. MK14 5DR
Tel: 01908 664518

Bio-Aura Enhanced Bio Energy Training
The Rookery, Newon, Northumberland, NE43 7UN
Tel: 01661 844899
Fax: 01661 844882
www.bi-aura.co.uk

Craniosacral Therapy Education Trust
10 Normington Close, Leigham Court Road, London. SW16 2QS
Tel/Fax: 07000 785778
www.cranio.co.uk

The Karuna Institute
Natsworthy Manor, Widecombe in the Moor, Nr Newton Abbot, Devon. TQ13
Tel/Fax: 01647 221 457
www.craniosacral.co.uk/kiet.htm

The College of Psychic Studies 16 Queensberry Place, London. SW7 2EB Tel: 020-7589 3292 Fax: 020-7589 2824 www.psychic-studies.org.uk	**The Bellmont Hypnotherapy Centre** **Professional Courses** The Belmont Centre, 46 Belmont Road, Ramsgate, Kent. CH1 7QG Tel: 01843 587929 Fax: 01843 587830 postbox@belmont-centre.co.uk
The College of Practical Homeopathy 760 High Road, North Finchley, London. N12 9QH Tel: 020-8445 6123 www.this.is/homeopathy	**The Guild of Naturopathic** **Iridologists (International)** 94 Grosvenor Road,London.SW1V 3LF Tel/Fax: 020-7821 0255 www.gni-international.org
London School of Classical **Homeopathy** School Office, 94 Green Dragon Lane, Winchmore Hill, London. N21 2NJ Tel/Fax: 020-8360 8757	**The Academy and Association of** **Systematic Kinesiology** 39 Browns Road, Surbiton, Surrey. KT5 8ST Tel: 020-8399 3215 Fax: 020-8390 1010 www.kinesiology.co.uk
London College of Shiatsu 25/27 Dalling Road, London. W6 0JD Tel: 020-8741 3323 www.londonschoolofshiatsu.com	**The International NLP Trainers** **Association Ltd (INLPTA)** PO Box 288, Fareham. PO16 0YG Tel: 01329 285353 Fax: 01329 285757 inlpta@aol.com
The British Institute of Homeopathy The Registrar, Cygnet House, Market Square, Staines, Middx. TW18 4RH Tel: 01784 440467 Fax: 01784 449887 www.britinsthom.com	**Inspire Partnership** 12 West Dean, Salisbury, Wilts.SP5 1JA Tel: 01794 340480 Fax: 01794 340476 Info@inspire-partnership.com
SACH School of Clinical and **Analytical Hypnotherapy** Tel: 0800 028 3071 SACHmail@aol.com www.sach-international.com	**International Teaching Seminars** 19 Widegate Street, London. E1 7HP Tel: 020-7247 0252 Fax: 020-7247 0242 www.itsnip.com
National College of Hypnosis and **Psycotherapy** 12 Cross Street,Nelson, Lancs.BB9 7EN Tel: 01282 699378 Fax: 01282 698633 www.nchp.clarets.co.uk	**John Seymour Associates** 17 Boyce Drive, Bristol. BS2 9XQ Tel: 0117-955 7827 www.johnseymour-nip.co.uk
The Atkinson-Ball College of Hypno- **Therapy and Hypno Healing** PO Box 70, Southport, Merseyside. PR8 3JB Tel/Fax: 01704 576285 www.hypnotapes.co.uk	**The National College of Hynosis and** **Psychotherapy** 12 Cross Street, Nelson. BB9 7EN Tel: 01282 699378 Fax: 01282-698633 www.nchp.clarets.co.uk

Rolando Toro School of Biodanza in the UK Director Patricia Martello. 48 Clifford Avenue, London. SW14 7BP Tel/Fax: 020-8392 1433 martello@biodanza.demon.co.uk	**Brightlife Ltd** The Gatehouse, Ballavoddan Manor, Andreas, Isle of Man. IM7 3HH Tel: 01624 880318 Fax: 01624 880967 www.brightlife.com
European College of Bowen Studies 38 Portway, Frome, Somerset. BA11 1QU Tel/Fax: 01373 461873 www.TheBowenTechnique.com	**Cariad Academy** PO Box 452A, Thames Ditton, Surrey. KT7 0WR TEl: 01932 269962 Fax: 01932 253220 academy@cariad.co.uk
The Bowen Association (UK) PO Box 4358, Dorchester, Dorset. DT2 7XX Tel: 07002 698324 www.bowen-technique.co.uk	**The College of Natural Therapy** 133 Gatley Road, Gatley, Cheadle, Cheshire. SK8 4PD Tel: 0161-491 4314 Fax: 0161-491 4190 www.colnat.co.uk
The Breema Center 6076 Claremont Avenue, Oakland,CA, 94618 USA. Tel: 001 510-428 0937 www.breema.com	**Institute of Phytobiophysics** Le Breton House, 10 St James Street, St Helier, Jersey. JE2 3QZ Tel: 01534 738737 Fax: 01534 618756
McTimoney College of Chiropractic The Clock House, 22-26 Ock Street, Abingdon. OX14 5SH Tel: 01235 523336	**The Radworth Centre** 20-26 South Street, Dorking, Surrey. RH4 2HQ Tel: 01306 742150 Fax: 01306 742163
The Oracle of Colour Pauline Wills, 9 Wyndale Avenue, London. NW9 9PT Tel/Fax:020-8204 7672 Pauline@oracleschool.fsnet.co.uk	**Stonebridge Associated Colleges** Dept PH, Efford Farm Business Park, Vicarage Road, Bude. EX23 8LT Tel: 01288 356300 Fax: 01288 355799 www.stonebridge.uk.com
Association of Natural Medicine 19A Collingwood Road, Witham, Essex. CM8 2DY Tel/Fax: 01376 502762	**Three Counties Training** 28 Longmead Liss, Hampshire. GU33 7DY Tel: 01730 893591 www.healingtouch.co.uk
Blackmores UK Willowtree Marina, West Quay Drive, Yeading, Middx. UB4 9TA Tel:020-8842 3956 Fax:020-8841 7557 blackmoresuk@intonet.co.uk	**College of Cranio-Sacral Therapy(CCST)** 9 St Georges Mews, Primrose Hill, London. NW1 8XE Tel: 020-7483 0120 www.ccst.co.uk

Martin NLP Broomfield Cottage, Hatfield Heath, Herts. CM22 7DZ Tel: 01279 731649 Fax: 01279 731699 www.martin-nlp.co.uk	**The Radionic & Radiesthesia Trust** Maperton, Wincanton, Somerset. BA9 8EH Tel: 01963 32651 Fax: 01963 32626
The British College Of Nutrition and Health Tel: 020-7372 4104 www.bcnh.co.uk	**Association of Reflexologists** 27 Old Gloucester Street, London. WC1N 3XX Tel: 0870 567 3320 www.reflexology.ogr/aor/
The College of Natural Nutrition 1 Halthaies, Bradninch,Devon.EX5 4LQ Tel/Fax: 01392 881091 cnn@globalnet.co.uk	**The British Reflexology Association** Monks Orchard, Whitbourne, Worcester. WR6 5RB Tel: 01886 821207 Fax: 01886 822017 www.britreflex.co.uk
Institute for Optimum Nutrition Blades Court, Deodar Road, London. SW15 2NU Tel: 020-8877 9993 Fax: 020-8877 9980 info@ion.ac.uk	**The Reflexologists' Society** General Secretary, PO Box 5422, Leicester. LE2 2YG Tel: 0870-607 3241
The Plaskett Nutritional Medicine College 14 Southgate Chambers, Launceston, Cornwall. Pl15 9DY Tel: 01566 773731 Fax: 01566 773741 www.pnmcollege.com	**The International Reiki and Healing Training Centre** 10 Beach Houses, Royal Crescent, Margate, Kent. CT9 5AL Tel: 01843 230377 Fax: 01843 230378 www.reiki-healing.com
Bodyharmonics Centre 54 Flecker's Drive, Cheltenham. GL51 5BD Tel 01242 582168 fax: 01242 694355	**School of Light** 12 Woodberry Grove, London.N12 0DL Tel: 020-8922 6857 Fax: 020-8446 2998 www.schooloflight.com
Malamute 42a Spital Hill, Gainsborough, Lincolnshire. DN21 1EG Tel: 01427 610652/0161 881 2764 www.malamute-uk.co.uk	**British School of Shiatsu-Do** The Shiatsu Place, 97-99 Seven Sisters Road, london. N7 7QP Tel: 020-7281 1412 Fax: 020-7281 1413 www.shiatsuplace.com
The School of Insight And Intuition Midford, Uxbridge Road, Hampton, Middlesex. TW12 1BD Tel: 020-8979 0940 Fax: 020-8255 8303 www.insightandintuition.com	**Thr European Shiatsu School** Central Office, Highbanks, Lockeridge, Marlborough, Wilts. SN8 4EQ Tel: 01672 513444 Fax: 01672 861459 www.shiatsu.org.uk

Alternative Aspects of Life
Advertising Rates

Display Adverts

Full page £180

2/3 page £140

1/3 page £85

1/6 page £45

Add 10% for typesetting display adverts.

Free inclusion of a Line Ad with every display rate order.

Line Ads (Small Classified)
Up to 10 words £10.00
11 - 20 words £15.00
21 - 30 words £21.00
31 - 40 words £28.00
41 - 50 words £34.00

If you wish to advertise in the next edition of this publication, please write to us at:
28 Matilda Way, Devizes, Wiltshire. SN10 2SH
Tel: +44 (0)1380 728940/739013
www.alternative-aspects.com
mail@alternative-aspects.com

Overview Map

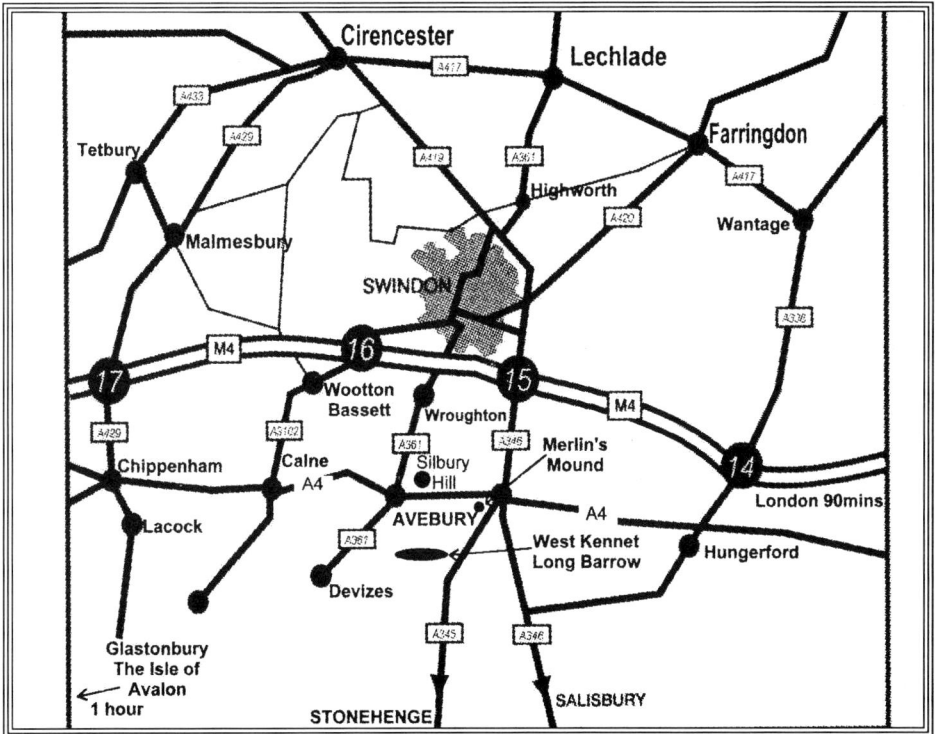

This overview map shows the wealth of historical places within a very small area. It is designed for approximate guidance when considering how best to plan your visit. Some of the main places of interest form a wonderful day trip from many major locations.

From London (only 1 1/2 hours drive) you can access some or Europes oldest and most sacred sites of worship.

Silbury Hill, constructed almost 5,000 years ago marks the largest man-made structure in Europe at that time.
Avebury Stone circle, erected some 4,500 years ago along with the avenue of stones can be walked today.
West Kennet Long Barrow, late Neolithic burial mound with chambers open to the public all year round. Constructed some 4,200 years ago.
Stonehenge needs no introduction, probably the most famous of all stone circles in the world and only 45mins from Avebury.
Glastonbury, legends of King Arthur, Avalon and biblical references makes this town and surrounding area a mystical must for anyone visiting this part of the world. So please enjoy our wonderful country side that surrounds immerses you in history.

Pagan and others dates

January
The January moon is known as... Wolf Moon, Quiet Moon, Snow Moon, Cold Moon, Chaste Moon, Disting Moon, Moon of Little Winter

Jan 6: Celtic day of the Three-fold Goddesses: Maiden, Mother and Crone
Jan 13: Festival of Saraavati in India. final witchcraft laws repealed in Austria 1787
Jan 14: Official confession of error by jurors of the Salem witch trials 1696
Jan 18: Theogamia of Hera (women's festival in honour of the goddess)
Jan 27: Roman day of the Earth Mother (Paganalia)
Jan 31: Dr Fian found guilty and executed for witchcraft in Scotland by personal order of King James VI (James I England) 1591

February
The February moon is known as... Ice Moon, Storm Moon, Horning Moon, Hunger Moon, Wild Moon, Red and Cleansing Moon, Quickening Moon, Solmanoth (Sun Month), Big Winter Moon

Feb 2: Imbolc (Groundhog Day)
Feb 7: Day of the moon goddess Selene. Death of Thomas Aquinas 1274
Feb 22: Roman 'Carista', day of family peace and accord
Feb 23: Roman 'Terminalia', honouring the god of boundaries 'Terminus'

March
The March moon is known as... The Storm Moon, Seed Moon, Moon of Winds, Plow Moon, Worm Moon, Hrethmonath (Hertha's Month), Lentzinmanoth (Renewal Month), Lenting Moon, Sap Moon, Crow Moon, Moon of the snowblind

March 1: Greek and Roman 'Matronalia', Festival of Hera and Juno Lucina. Celtic Feast of Rhiannon. Preliminary hearings in the Salem Witch trials held1692
March 14: 'The Diasia' Greek festival to ward of poverty. Jacques de Molay (head of the Knights Templar in France) retracts his confession of herasy before being burned at the stake
March 17: Festival of Astarte in Canaan. Roman 'Liberalia' womens festival of freedom. Eleanor Shaw and Mary Phillips executed in England for bewitching a woman and her two children 1705
March 18: Sheelah's Day Irish time to honour Sheelah-Na-Gig the goddess of fertility
March 19: Elizabethan statute against witchcraft enacted 1563
March 20: Egyptian Spring harvest festival honouring Isis
March 21: Spring Equinox Festival of Kore (Demeter in Greece)
March 22-27: Greek 'Hilaria' Festivals to honour Cybele
March 23: Roman 'Quinquatria' Birthday of Athena/Minerva
March 24: Arrest of Florence Newton, one of the witches to be burned in Ireland 1661

March 29: Greek 'Delphinia of Artemis'. Tibetan time for expulsion of the demons of bad luck

March 30: 'Feast of Eostre' German goddess of Spring and rebirth

March 31: Roman 'Festival of Luna' in honour of the moon goddess. Last witch trial in Ireland at Magee Island 1711

April

The April moon is known as... Growing Moon, Hare Moon, Seed Moon, Planting Moon, Planters Moon, Budding Trees Moon, Eastermonath (Eostre Month), Ostarmanoth, Pink Moon, Green Grass Moon.

April 1: Indian 'Festival of Kali'. Roman 'Fortuna Virilis of Venus'. Egyptian 'Day of Hathor'. Death of Richard Napier

April 5: Roman festival for good luck, paying homage to the goddess Fortuna. Trial of Alice Samuel found guilty. along with her husband and daughter. of bewitching the wife of Sir Henry Cromwell and several village children 1593

April 11: Armenain 'Day of Anahit' the moon goddess of love. Burning of Major Weir (Scottish sorcerer, condemned by his own word)

April 15: Egyptian 'Festival of Bast'

April 19: Conviction of witches at the second of four trials at Chelmsford England 1579

April 22: Babylonian 'Festival of Ishtar'

April 28-May 3: Roman 'Floralia' 'Festival of Flora and Venus'

May

The May moon is known as... Hare moon, Merry Moon, Dyad Moon, Bright Moon, Flower Moon, Frogs Return Moon, Thrimilcmonath (Thrice-Milk Month), Sproutkale, Winnemanoth (Joy Month), Planting Moon.

May 1: Beltane. 'Rowan Witch Day' in honour of the Finnish goddess Rauni

May 4: Irish 'Sacred Thorn Tree Day'

May 11: Massachussetts Bay Colony Puritans ban Christmas celebrations because they are too Pagan 1659

May 23: Roman 'Rosalia' Rose festival of Flora and Venus

May 24: Birth of Artemis/diana

May 26: Chinese 'Day of Chin-hua-fu-jen'

May 27: Final confession of witchcraft by Isobel Gowdie, Scotland 1662

June

The June moon is known as... Mead Moon, Moon of Horses, Lovers' Moon, Strong Sun Moon, Honey Moon, Aerra Litha (Befire Lithia), Brachmanoth (break Month), Strawberry Moon, Rose Moon, Moon of Making Fat.

June 1: Witchcraft act of 1563 takes effect in England

June 2: Babylonian 'Shapatu (sabbat) of Ishtar

June 10: Hanging of Bridget Bishop, first to die in the Salem Witch trials 1692

June 11: James I witchcraft act replaces 1563 mandate with strict penalties 1604. James

I law is repealed in 1736 and replaced with a law against 'pretending' to perform witch-craft, which was in turn repealed in 1951

June 15: Margaret Jones (doctor) becomes the first person to be executed as a Witch in the Massachusetts Bay Colony when several of her patients die 1648

June 16: Egyptian 'Night of the Teardrop' Feast of the Waters of the Nile, in honour of the goddess Isis

June 21: Summer Solstice British 'Day of Cerridwen'. Irish dedication to the faery goddess Aine of Knockaine. Northern European 'Day of the Green Man'

June 22: Final witchcraft law in England repealed 1951

July

The July moon is known as... Hay Moon, Wort Moon, Moon of Claiming, Moon of Blood (mosquitoes), Blessing Moon, Meadmonat (Meadow Month), Hewimanoth (Hay Month), Fallow Moon, Buck Moon, Thunder Moon.

July 5: Conviction of witches at the third of four trials at Chelmsford England 1589

July 10: Day of Hel (Anglo Saxon/Norse goddess) and Cerridwen (Celtic goddess)

July 17: Egyptian birthday of Isis

July 18: Egyptian birthday of Nephthys

July 19: Egyptian New Year. 'Opet Festival' (marriage of Isis and Osiris). Roman celebration of Venus and Adonis. Rebecca Nurse hanged in Salem Massachusetts 1692

July 22: Northamptonshire Witches condemned 1612

July 27: Belgian 'Procession of the Witches'. Jennet Preston becomes the first 'Malkin Tower' witch to be hung 1612

July 29: Agnes Waterhouse (one of the Chelmsford Witches) is hanged 1566

August

The August moon is known as... Corn Moon, Barley Moon, Dispute Moon, Weodmonath (Vegetation Month), Harvest Moon, Moon When cherries Turn Black.

Aug 1: Celtic 'Festival of New Bread' Lammas. Aztec 'Festival of Xiuhtecuhtli' god of the calendar

Aug 20: Execution of the Lancashire Witches 1612

Aug 29: Egyptian birthday of Hathor, New Year's Day

September

The September moon is known as... Harvest Moon, Wine Moon, Singing Moon, Sturgeon Moon, Haligmonath (Holy Month), Witumanoth (Wood Month), Moon When Deer Paw the Earth.

Sept 8: Tibetan 'Water Festival' in honour of water sprites

Sept 9: Else Pfraum sentenced to death for witchcraft in Germany 1603

Sept 13-14: Egyptian 'Ceremony of Lighting the Fire' in honour of Mephthys and the spirits of the dead

Sept 14: Phillip IV of France orders the arrest of the French Templars 1306

Sept 19: Egyptian (Alexandrian) day long fast to honour Thoth as god of wisdom and magic

Sept 22: Autum Equinox Mabon. Sumerian death of Tiamat

October

The October moon is known as... Blood Moon, Harvest Moon, Shedding Moon, Winterfelleth (Winter Coming), Windermanoth (Vintage Month), Falling Leaf Moon, Ten Colds Moon, Moon of the Changing season.

Oct 7: Sumerian New Year in honour of the goddesses Ishtar and Astarte

Oct 12: Roman 'Fortuna Redux' celebration for happy journeys. Birthday of Aleister Crowley

Oct 13: Jacques de Molay and other French Templars arrested by order of King Phillip IV 1306

Oct 18: British 'Great Horn Fair' in honour of the Horned God

Oct 25: Chinese 'Festival of Han Lu' Moon and Harvest goddess. Jacques de Molay first interrogated after Templar arrest 1306

Oct 26: Egyptian 'Festival of Hathor'. De Molay and 31 other Templars confess to herasy, all these confessions are later recanted 1306

The late October moon is known as... Blue Moon, Moon of the dead, Hunting Moon, Ancestor Moon, Hunters Moon.

Oct 28-Nov 2: Egyptian 'Isia' celebrating the search and recovery of Osiris

Oct 29: Iroquois 'Feast of the Dead'

Oct 31: Celtic 'Samhain' (Celtic Feast of the Dead). Egyptian 'Feast of Sekhmet and Bast'. Indian 'Festival of Dasehra' celebrating the battle of Rama and Kali against Ravana the demon.

November

The November moon is known as... Snow Moon, Dark Moon, Fog Moon, Beaver moon, Mourning Moon, Blotmonath (Sacrifice Month), Herbismanoth (Harves Month), Mad Moon, Moon of Storms, Moon When Deer Shed Antlers

Nov 3: Egyptian last day of 'Isia', rebirth of Osiris. Petronella de Meath is executed in the first recorded witch burning in Ireland 1324

Nov 6: Babylonian birthday of Tiamat

Nov 8: Shinto 'Fuigo Matsuri' festival in honour of Inari goddess of the Kitchen Range. Sentencing of witches in Zugarramurdi trial (most famous witch trial in the Basque region) 1610. Bessi Dunlop condemned in Scotland 1576

Nov 9-10: Scottish 'Night of Nicnevin'

Nov 16: Greek 'Night of Hecate'. Egyptian'Festival of Bast'

Nov 22: Pope Clement issues bull Pastoralis Praeminentiae calling for monarchs in west-

December

The December moon is known as... Cold Moon, Oak Moon, Wolf moom, Moon of Long nights, Long Nights Moon, Aerra Geola (Month Before yule), Wintermonat (Winter month), Heilagmanoth (Holy Month), Big winter Moon, Moon of Popping Trees

Dec 1: Greek and Roman 'Day of Pallas Athene/Minerva'
Dec 5: Death if Aleister Crowley 1947
Dec 8: Mayan 'festival of Ixchel'. Egyptian 'Festival of Neith'. Greek 'Astraea' dedicated to the goddess Astraea, deity of justice
Dec 10: Roman 'Festival of Lux Mundi' (Light of the World)
Dec 21: Celtic 'Winter Solstice' Festival of the Stars. Egyptian return of Osiris to Isis
Dec 23 : Egyptian 'Day of Hathor'. Egyptian 'Night of Lamps' final entombment of Osiris
Dec 24: Anglo Saxon 'Modresnach' (Mother Night). German 'Night of the Mothers'
Dec 26: Egyptian birthday of Horus
Dec 27: Norse birthday of Freyja
Dec 31: Roman 'Day of Hecate'. Egyptian 'Lucky day of Sekhmet'. Scottish 'Hogmanay'. Welsh 'Faery of the Van'. sicilian celebration of Strenia, goddess of gifts. French celebration of Dame Abonde for presents. Mexican 'Wishing Night'.

Whatever your faith or following we hope you have found the information both interesting and helpful. Many interpretaions of God or God's can be found throughout history but whatever form, if any, your belifes take it would seem that interpretaions of a greater truth is the main cause for conflict. I often use the line at my lectures "The bible is a great book...shame the church got hold of it". The idea that the earth is a living entity and we are part of the eco-structure makes perfect sense. As for an intelligence behind it all, I cannot think that the whole of creation and evolution is the result of random accidents. If we were ever to find what the true meaning of God is or life, I suspect it would never be understood, even while it stared us in the face. Please feel free to come visit the web site, have a look and if the download area is up and running you can have a look at other articals written by one of the authors. Paganisum is one of many subjects covered on our site, if you want to become part of a greater gathering of complimentary souls then why not join us. See display ad in this publication for www.alternative-aspects.com.

Parting Thoughts

Avebury is only one of many sites around the world that have what could be described as a mysterious past. Easter Island, Machu Picchu, Nazca lines, the great Pyramids and many more such sites have defied the efforts of a complete explanation. By simply willing to consider every fact, every possibility, without any prior opinions by past conditioning we may begin to evaluate the past more objectively.

Copernicus dared to question the Church's view of the universe, suggesting that the Earth revolved around the Sun. The church (none of which were qualified to comment) condemned him as a heretic. It took almost 400 years for his observations to be accepted as fact. In principal we have not travelled much further from those close-minded days.

The advances made in parapsychology, physics, chemistry and medicine are slowly demonstrating that in many ways our ancient ancestors knew more than we give them credit for. The Quantum observation of all the areas mentioned above and the quest to investigate our galactic neighbours seems to be demonstrating a reality that moves ever closer to explaining the more unusual aspects of life.

Why should not the civilisations of the distant past have had access to knowledge that we find beyond our present understanding ? Could they not have experienced periods of enlightenment during which the subtle fields that permeate all life was revealed to them ? Is there any reason why the moments of illumination or profound intuition resulting in the sudden explosion of genius within the life of a person should not have occurred many times in the life of the human race ?

This does not advocate the false interpretation of evidence as we see it. It allows us to retain the possibility that mythology, myths, legends and magic have a stronger base than mere hearsay. There are many questions still to be addressed and one could, and many do, spend a lifetime trying to find answers. It is far better for you to choose your own path than the road that someone else recommends for you. Our guide has been a small contribution towards the a journey that in the mist of a crowded world must be taken alone.

We sincerely hope you continue to grow in your own way and are able to accept that others have to do the same. Stop thinking of what man is, observation of just the physical will never give us all the answers, start to consider what we may become.

We thought it may also be helpful to give you some of the terms you may come across when reading other archaeological books and guides.

Avenue A processional or ritual way, usually marked out by two parallel banks.

Beakers Characteristic pottery (*c*.2500-1900BC) of Neolithic invaders known as "Beaker Folk".

Bronze Age Period of Bronze technology, beginning in Britain *c*.2000BC.

Causeway Camp/Enclosure Mid-Neolithic hilltop settlement surrounded by irregular banks and ditches.

Cursus Mid-Neolithic linear earthwork with parallel banks and unknown ritual purpose, up to 9.6km long.

Derevel-Rimbury A mid-Bronze age culture.

Druids Celtic priesthood of the later Iron Age, too late to have a role in Stonehenge or Avebury.

Grooved Ware Late Neolithic pottery decorated with striped panels, often associated with henges.

Henge Circular or oval late Neolithic/early Bronze Age ritual earthwork, sometimes with a stone circle.

Long Barrow Long Neolithic mound with functions as a burial place, temple and marker of tribal territory.

Megalith *mega*=big, *lith*=stone.

Mortuary Enclosure/House Place safe from scavengers where bodies were defleshed before burial of bones.

Neolithic The New Stone age from the first settled farmers to the arrival of bronze technology. Dated in Britain to *c*4500-2000 BC.

Round Barrow Circular mound (five main types) covering a prestigious Bronze Age burial.

Sarsens Natural sandstone blocks found lying on Cretaceous chalk downs and used for megaliths.

Solstice Longest or shortest day of the year.

Stone Circle Neolithic/Bronze Age ritual arrangement of megaliths, often not strictly circular.

Trilithon Three large stones arranged like a doorway of two uprights and a lintel, as at Stonehenge.

Wessex The southern English counties of Berkshire, Dorset, Hampshire, Somerset and Wiltshire.

Windmill Hill A famous mid-Neolithic site.

We hope you have enjoyed this publication and look forward to bringing you further "Unusual Aspects" of various sites of interest. Maybe there are places you know that by using the principals contained here you can make any day out both educational and fun.

If you have found this publication interesting and informative we thank you. A unique opportunity exists for those who would like to organise with a few friends a guided tour of the stones. As local authors we can and do accompany visitors around the stones. Our alternative views may not be in keeping with traditional ideas but we think you will find it most entertaining.

To contact us for further information on this use our E-mail or leave your contact information with a member of staff at The Red Lion. rob333@btinternet.com Or alistairh@lycos.com

NOTES